St. Michael's Church

Art & Artefacts

compiled by

Madeleine Maher

Published by
Spirit Publications,
For
St. Michael's Church,
Marine Road,
Dun Laoghaire,
Co. Dublin,
Ireland.

Text by Madeleine Maher
Layout and Design by Vivienne Maher
Photography by Vivienne Maher

ISBN 0-9546237-0-3

Printed in Ireland by ColourBooks Ltd.,
105, Baldoyle Industrial Estate,
Dublin 13.

Every effort has been made to be as accurate as possible. Any relevant information not included would be welcome.

St. Michael's Church,
Marine Road,
Dun Laoghaire.

29th September, 2003
Feast of St. Michael Archangel – Parish Patron

FOREWORD

I am indeed pleased to write the foreword for this publication "The Art and Artefacts" of our Parish Church as researched and compiled by Madeleine Maher of our Parish.

The Holy Father's Intentions in the Book of the Apostleship of Prayer for July 2002 reads "That Artists do all that they can to help the women and men of today to rediscover the signs of God's Providential Love in Creation." That intention is being fulfilled in our Parish Church.

The foundation stone of our Parish Church, St. Michael's, Dun Laoghaire, was laid by His Grace, Archbishop Dermot Ryan, on Sunday 1st October 1972. The Church was officially opened and blessed on Sunday 7th October 1973 by Dr. Ryan.

It was looked upon then – as quite a different style of Church than that which was to be seen anywhere else in Ireland or even in the world. The Architect, Pearse McKenna, now gone to his reward, gave to the people of this community something quite unique in style, design and furnishing. Over the years many artists have added much to bring out the real spiritual heritage which we enjoy today. The works of the various artists which you can study and enjoy in this volume attract people, not only from the greater Dublin area but from all over Ireland and abroad.

John Paul II in his letter to artists said – society needs artists just as it needs scientists, technicians, workers, professional people, witnesses of the faith, teachers, fathers and mothers, who ensure the growth of the person and the development of the community by means of that supreme art form which is the art of education. Within the vast cultural panorama of each nation, artists have their unique place. Obedient to their inspiration in creating works both worthwhile and beautiful, they not only enrich the cultural heritage of each nation and of all humanity – but they also render an exceptional social service in favour of the common good.

Here in St. Michael's Parish Church, Dun Laoghaire, the particular vocation of the individual artists decided the unique contribution each has made to the beautifying of this House of God. There is indeed, evident in our Parish Church an ethic, even a spirituality, of artistic service which contributes in its own way to the life and renewal of our people, and of thousands of visitors from abroad, who come here to pray and study the various architectural, sculptural and artistic detail of this House of God.

The magnificent contribution by the artists is only made possible by the commissions and donations of our wonderful parishioners, patrons and donors who have sponsored these works and to whom we are all individually and collectively forever indebted.

My gratitude to Madeleine Maher who meticulously and generously put this volume together, which will act as a study guide to our understanding and appreciation of the richness of our Christian heritage and of the beauty of our Church. May this work and our whole lives always be directed to the praise of God and the growth of His Kingdom.

Patrick J. Mangan P.P.

Patrick J. Mangan, P.P.
Dun Laoghaire.

Acknowledgements

To my husband and family, and to all who gave information or help of any kind to assist in the compilation of this book, grateful thanks. Thanks also to our Parish Priest, Father Patrick Mangan, for his encouragement and resourcefulness.

Special thanks to Michael O'Donovan, of Patrick O'Donovan & Son, Funeral Directors Ltd., 5/6 Church Place, Sallynoggin, Co. Dublin, for his generous sponsorship.

Contents

Appendices:

MAIN DOORS, ST. MICHAEL ABOVE THE MAIN DOORS, BRONZE DOOR HANDLES. ARTIST IMOGEN STUART R.H.A.

Imogen Stuart's description of the artwork:

"Like the old church in Dun Laoghaire which was burnt down, the new one is dedicated to St. Michael the Archangel. The Hebrew word Michael means: Who is like God. There are many references to St. Michael in the Old Testament. He is the leader of the heavenly army, carrying a lance and fighting the dragon who, traditionally, symbolises Satan. Above the main door of the church I show him as the slayer of Evil. The work was executed in sheetcopper in a technique similar to copper-roofing. All my work on St. Michael's Church is dedicated to Angels. The fixed panel of the beaten copper main doors show an angel surrounded by the traditional attributes of angels: palms – musical instruments – scripture scrolls – wings – and a flaming sword and weighing scales for the last Judgement. Above you can see Christ in Glory surrounded by angels.

The handrails of the main doors are decorated with the symbols of the four evangelists. These are ancient traditional images. Their origin is first mentioned in the great vision of Ezekiel prophesying the evangelists and first seen on churches of the 4th Century. Each gospel in the Book of Kells and Book of Durrow is illuminated on its beginning page with the image of an evangelist and his relevant symbol: The angel or man symbolises St. Matthew, describing Christ's life on earth. St. Luke who so intensely describes Christ's sacrificial death is symbolised as the bull/ox. St. Mark, symbolised by the Lion, emphasises in his gospel the power of the resurrection and the conquering of death. St. John is symbolised as the eagle who stresses in his gospel Christ's ascension into heaven.

The short handles on the side doors are again decorated with music making angels.

The bronzecast altar bell is inspired by the old Irish ones. The simplified shape of the handle is constructed from two little altar boys having a tug-of-war."

PAINTING – BAPTISM. ARTIST - PETER CASSIDY.

Peter Cassidy's description of the painting:

"In this painting the principal theme of Baptism is indicated by the pouring of water, the water of life from the hands of God.

Ezekiel 36.25. **'I shall pour clean water over you and you will be cleansed'.**

Luke 3.6. **'he will baptise you with the holy spirit and with fire'.**

Parallel with this, the sense of creation is suggested by sunrise.

Gen. 1.3. **'God said 'let there be light', and there was light'.**

On the left the crucified figure is suspended on a truncated tree which is seen as a transfixed hand. These symbols of the abuse of God and of nature are balanced on the right by the angelic figure derived from a Tieoplo mural, (an Italian artist of 18th century), which acts as a herald to the good news of Baptism, and the resurrection that that promises.

Romans. 8: 22/23 'the whole creation until this time, has been groaning in labour pains,….. waiting in eagerness for our bodies to be set free'.

The painting is dedicated to the memory of Diarmuid Larkin ANCA."

TAPESTRY OF OUR LADY AND THE CHILD JESUS
ARTISTS - EOIN AND PAT BUTLER.

Eoin and Pat Butler's description of the tapestry:

"The tapestry in the baptistery area of St. Michael's Church by Eoin and Pat Butler is composed of five panels and is set into a bronze cruciform frame.

The main centre panel shows Our Lady presenting her divine Son to the world, inviting all of us to share with her the celebration of His coming, ever mindful of the Holy Cross, the Christian symbol of our salvation, flanked by attending angels on the two side panels.

In the top panel we find the symbol of the Holy Spirit, who remains with us always, and most especially in the Divine Word. The symbol of the Trinity reminds us that Christ is one with the Father and the Spirit.

The bottom panel – we the people of God praying to Christ through the intercession of His Mother, and living and fulfilling our lives in the love and involvement of His holy church."

THE ORGAN

The organ, by Rieger of Austria, was installed in 1974 under the advice of Gerard Gillen, who at that time was Lecturer of Music at UCD, (later appointed Titular Organist of the Pro-Cathedral in 1976). It is designed in the strict neo classical style. The organ has 25 stops distributed over two manuals and pedals and totalling 1726 pipes. The pipes of the second manual are rendered expressive by the action of glass louvres which are a distinctive feature of this organ. The Spanish trumpet pipes are arranged horizontally – also a distinctive feature. An unusual feature, in Ireland at least, is the Zimbelstern, a rotating star with bells attached.
(See Appendix 6 for Organ Stops List).

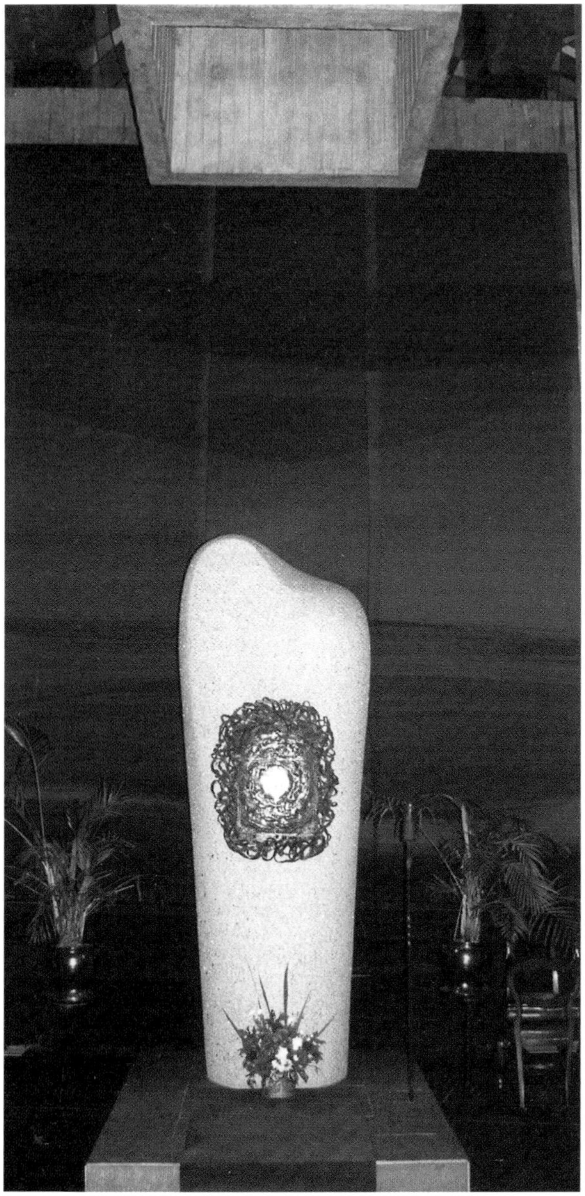

TAPESTRY ON THE SANCTUARY WALL.

ARTISTS - EOIN AND PAT BUTLER.

Eoin and Pat Butler's description of the tapestry:

"In essence, the tapestry is a prayer that rejoices in the Risen Christ. 'Let us thank God for giving us the victory through Our Lord Jesus Christ'.
The work itself is not intended to be a showpiece.
Through the warmth of its textured colour, it seeks to enhance our sense of the sacred, the wonder and awe we experience at the mystery of God's presence when we assemble here for public worship, or for private prayer.
The richness, powerfulness and basic associations of red itself should help us reflect upon Christ's death, and His triumphant resurrection. Our prayer begins in grief, as the dark red texture invites us into Gethsemene and on to Calvary.
Passing gently into lighter shades, the tapestry colour – patterns converge in a rhythmic dance that symbolises our joy in the Resurrection.
'You are sad now, but I shall see you again, and your hearts will be full of joy, and that joy no one shall take from you'. (John 16,22)."

THE HIGH ALTAR, TABERNACLE PILLAR, AMBO, SEAT AND BAPTISMAL FONT

SCULPTOR – THE LATE MICHAEL BIGGS. 1928 – 1993.

In a TV programme, ***Michael Biggs, Artist in Stone,*** (RTE 1973) in which Michael Biggs can be seen working on these pieces, he said "There are five stones, an Altar, a Font, a pillar for the Tabernacle, an Ambo and this Seat for the priest. I have the idea that if you are going to use stone you should take a lump straight out of the quarry and shape that. If things are to have a spiritual quality they must first of all have a material quality."

Of the Altar he said: "looking at this completely in a professional way, and providing what I hope might have significance for people, I think the idea is that the Mass is a miracle. This table is not just a table, it has to be more than that. It is the location of the miracle. It is the spot where it takes place. I think you have to try and express that in some way and you don't express that by any sort of merely decorative thing, you only hamper it."

The Altar, Tabernacle Pillar, Ambo, Seat and Baptismal Font are made from granite taken from Walsh's Quarry, in Ballyedmonduff, Sandyford, Co. Dublin. They are mounted on Liscanor Slate from County Clare.

All of the work done by Michael Biggs was hand carved. He wanted to release the form in the stone and let it speak for itself of the glory and splendour of God.
He was especially renowned for his lettering.

The foundation stone laid in the south wall of the Church, by His Grace Dermot Ryan, Archbishop of Dublin, on Sunday 1st October 1972, was designed by the late Michael Biggs and carved by Thomas Glendon, Letter Cutter and Sculptor.

THE ABSTRACT STAINED GLASS WINDOWS AND PORCH WINDOWS

MURPHY DEVITT STUDIOS.

John A. Devitt's Description of the Windows:

"The stained glass in St. Michael's was made at Murphy Devitt Studios, Blackrock, Co. Dublin, at the time the Church was built. The windows were made entirely with antique French Glass.

The abstract design relates to the soaring spirit. The roof appears to be separated from the main structure. The large white shapes of glass are sparse at the extremities and come closer in a more agitated form at the Centre of the windows at the top. The upright windows leading to the horizontal tops show a beginning of this movement. The glass is mostly in various grey antiques and is relieved by tints of white and strong notes of selenium orange and yellow antique glass.

The side windows in the sanctuary are also in French Antique Glass and are an abstract lacing design which is uniquely modern.

The Porch windows are made of 1" thick French Antique Dalle-du-Verre Glass, cast in stone filled resin to give surface texture.

The windows were designed to enhance the stark engineering structural quality of the building and were not to be in competition with any other surface decoration."

TABERNACLE, CRUCIFIX AND SANCTUARY LAMP.
ARTIST – THE LATE RICHARD ENDA KING. (1943 - 1995)

Description given by Mary King, widow of the late Richard Enda King.

"Crucifix: The corpus of the Crucifix is fabricated in cast bronze, vitreous enamelled. The shaft of the cross is in wrought copper fabricated from one continuous length of copper section. This involved the heating of the copper and then whilst it was hot, twisting it into the required shape.

Tabernacle: The theme of the Tabernacle is as follows:

"....the angel of Yahweh appeared to him [Moses] in the shape of a flame of fire, coming from the middle of a bush ......and God called him from the middle of the bush. ' Moses! Moses! ' he said. 'Here I am,' he answered. 'Come no nearer', he said 'for the place on which you stand is holy ground. I am the God of your father,' he said, 'the God of Abraham, the God of Isaac and the God of Jacob.' Exodus 3:1.

The tabernacle surround is fabricated in wrought copper, with the centrepiece containing the doors, completed in beaten copper, vitreous enamelled. (This centre was originally also surrounded by wrought copper which was removed some years after its installation)

Sanctuary Lamp: This is also fabricated in wrought copper.

Vitreous enamel is a process where a mixture of glass powder and coloured oxide is applied to metal and kiln fired at about 840 degrees centigrade so that it fuses with the metal".

Also the work of Richard Enda King:
The Tabernacle at the rear of the Pillar was used in the temporary church, which is now the Boylan Community Centre.
The stepped flower stands (with vases inserted) are made in wrought metal. The altar and paschal candlesticks are also made in wrought metal.

Tabernacle behind Tabernacle Pillar

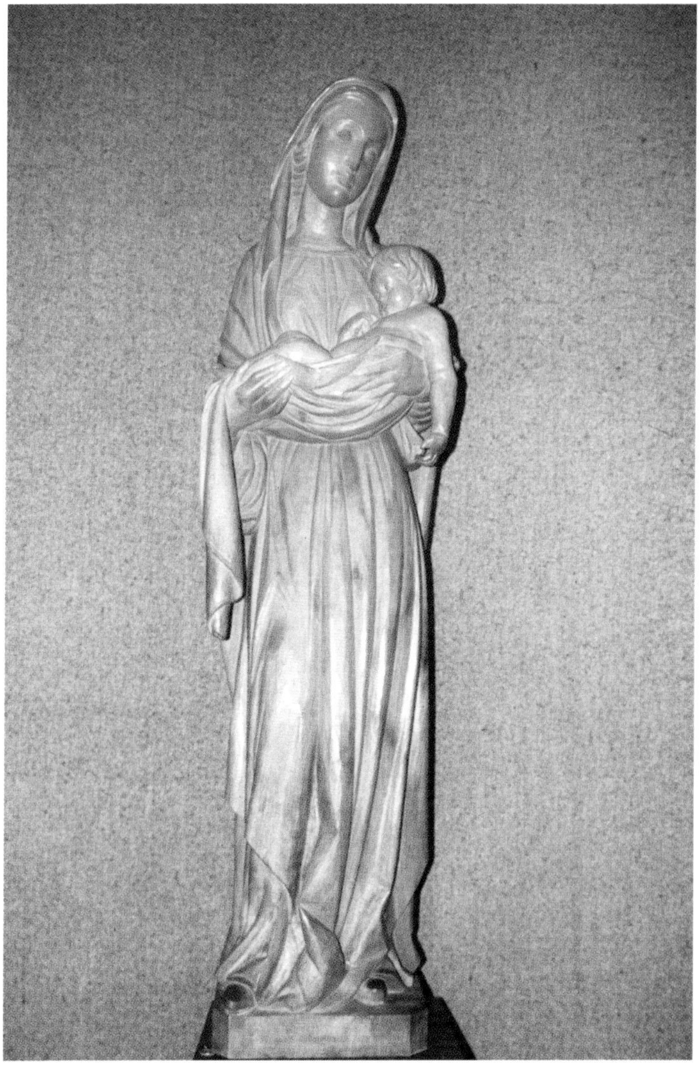

The Statues of The Sacred Heart and of Our Lady
were carved in Oberammergau.

The Statue of St. Thérèse of Lisieux
(For information on the life of St. Thérèse see Appendix 1).

The Bell near the Statue of St. Thérèse.
Artist – Unknown.
Description: Solid Brass. Inscription around the Bell (in Latin) loosely translated, gives its message: "Whoever touches me shall hear my voice".

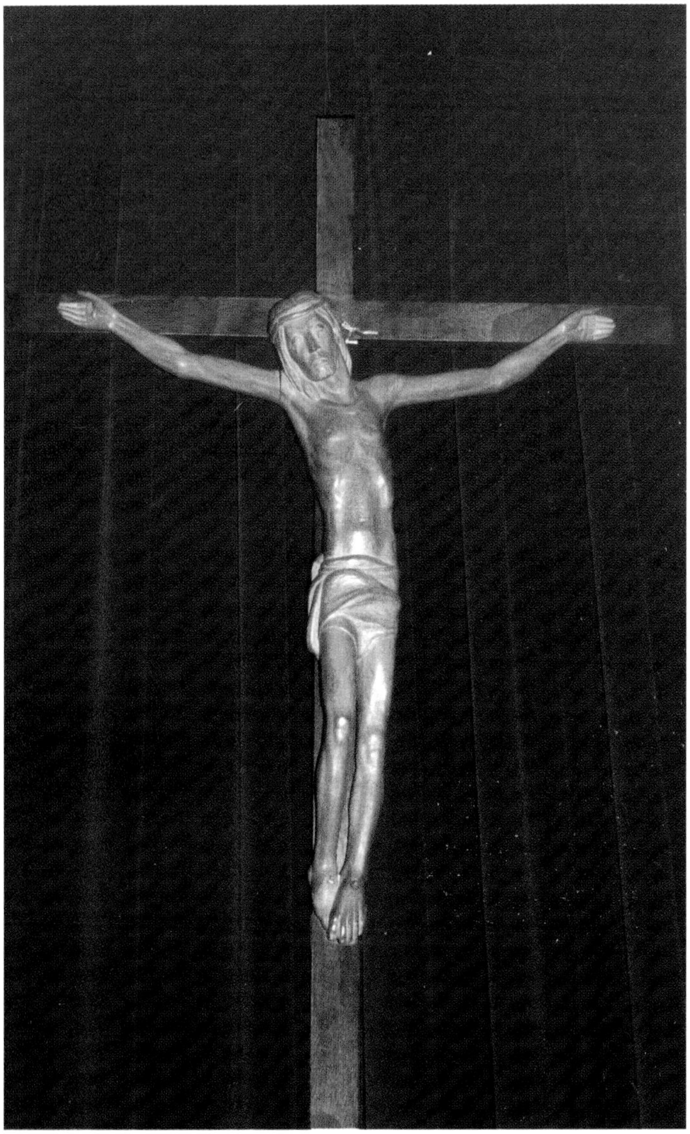

The Crucifix (in the Mortuary).

This was used in the temporary church, (now the Boylan Community Centre), while the new church was being built.

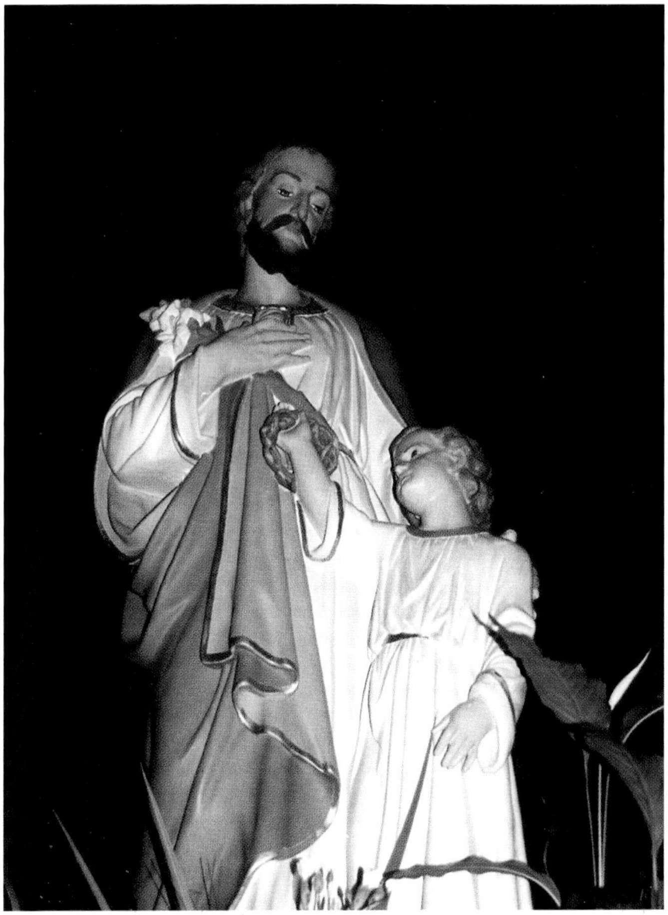

The Statue of St. Joseph

The Picture of The Divine Mercy.
(For information on the picture see Appendix 2).

The Statue of Blessed Edmund Ignatius Rice is the work of Dublin Sculptor, Peter Grant A.N.C.A. (1915 – 2003). This statue is a copy of the four foot model, used by Peter Grant, for the ten foot carving in limestone of the Rice Monument at Rice Street, Callan, Co. Kilkenny. The model was exhibited at the Royal Hibernian Academy.
(For information on the life of Blessed Edmund Ignatius Rice see Appendix 3).

The Statue of Blessed Charles of Mount Argus is the work of a local Sculptor and Potter, Peter Joseph Brennan A.N.C.A. (1916 – 1995).
(For information on the life of Blessed Charles of Mount Argus see Appendix 4).

Emblem Hanging On The Wall Behind The Statue of Blessed Charles Of Mount Argus:
This wall hanging displays the emblem/logo used for the visit of Pope John Paul II to Ireland in 1979.

The Statue of St. Anthony of Padua was carved in Oberammergau. (For information on the life of St. Anthony see Appendix 5).

THE PAINTING ABOVE CONFESSIONAL.

This picture was painted by a local artist, (name unknown) who asked if it could be hung in the Church during an Art Festival Week in Dun Laoghaire some years ago.

THE PLAQUE OF JESUS AND OUR LADY
(above the holy water font)

ARTIST – IAN STUART

This plaque is carved in mahogany and represents the fourth station, Jesus meets his Mother.

THE HOLY WATER FONTS
(at the two side entrances).

These are made of bronze and have the imprint of a fish. A fish was the symbol used by Christians in Roman times proclaiming their belief in Jesus Christ Son of God.

THE STATIONS OF THE CROSS.
ARTIST – THE LATE MADAME JAMMET.

The Stations of the Cross were carved in mahogany by Madame Jammet.

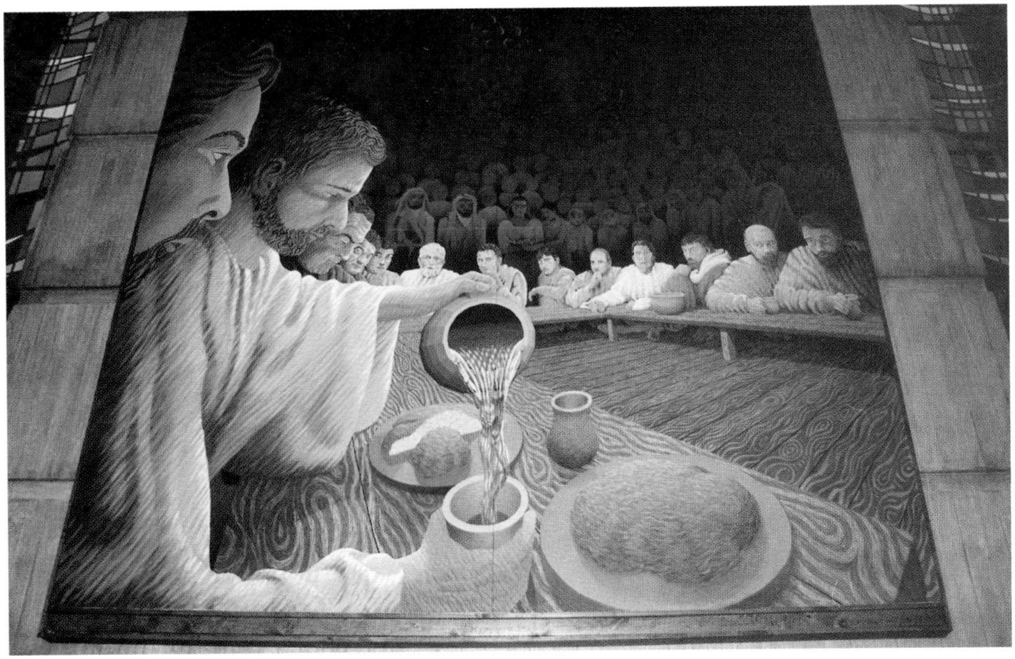

PAINTING : THE LAST SUPPER (1998)

ARTIST - PETER CASSIDY

Peter Cassidy's description of the painting:

"The main inspiration for The Last Supper is taken both from **John's Gospel Chapter 13 through to 15,** together with ideas as to the shape and arrangement of the table based on modern Jewish historical research by the Biblical Institute of Jerusalem. This suggests that a typical formal meal such as the Passover would have been grouped around a low 'U' shaped table with people reclining, (generally to their left), on cushions on the ground. The host for such a meal would not sit at the centre of the 'U', but rather at the 2nd place from the end of the left arm of the 'U' as you face the painting. Here we find Christ in the act of pouring the wine of the first Eucharist **'This is my blood, the blood of the covenant poured out for many'. (Mk. 14 : 24).** Within the image of the pouring wine Christ's crucified body is suggested, **'For my flesh is real food, and my blood is real drink' (J. 6 : 55).**

The apostles are reclining around the table. The first apostle on the left as you view the painting is John. **'The disciple whom Jesus loved was reclining next to Jesus'. (J. 13 : 23).** In our tradition this would be the place of honour but in the Jewish tradition of the time the place of honour beside the host is now thought to be on the hosts left. We might expect to see Peter here but we do not. Peter is not seated close to Jesus for as John's Gospel describes earlier during the meal, before the moment depicted in this painting, **'Simon Peter signed to him (John)' (J. 13 : 24)** when telling John to ask Christ who the betrayer might be. Therefore Peter must not have been seated beside Jesus and was not able to question Jesus directly, so instead he signed to John to ask Jesus who His betrayer was. Jesus had said in reply to that question **'It is the one to whom I give the piece of bread that I dip in the dish. And when he had dipped the piece of bread he gave it to Judas' (J. 13: 26),** and so in this painting Judas is also seated beside Jesus but on His left, to Jesus right as we view the painting.

'I am the vine you are the branches' (J. 15 : 5)

John
'The disciple whom Jesus loved was
reclining next to Jesus', (J.13.23).

Christ
'This is my blood, the blood of the covenant
poured out for many', (Mk. 14 : 24)

Judas
'It is the one to whom I give the
piece of bread' (J.13 : 26)

Mary of Magdala
'I wish to celebrate the Passover
with my disciples' (Mt. 26 : 18)

Christ crucified within the wine
'For my flesh is real food, and my
blood is real drink' (J. 6: 55)

Peter
'if anyone wants to be first he must make himself
last of all and servant of all' (Mk. 9 :35)

In this painting Peter is found at the end of the opposite arm of the 'U' at the extreme right of the painting. His location here is supposition for this place would be regarded as the lowest placing at the table but may well be very appropriate considering the incident earlier in the meal when Jesus washes the apostles feet and Peter argues with Christ about it, now it may be that he is pondering Christ's words, **'if anyone wants to be first he must make himself last of all and servant of all' (Mk. 9 : 35)**

Behind the twelve are representatives of all humanity men women and children for we are all called to share in that Eucharist. Included in this group is Mary of Magdala who is carrying a plate of grapes. Christ said **'I am the vine you are the branches' (J.15 : 5)**, and so the people become the vines in the painting above. In the painting there is a relationship between the background and the foreground. The grapes above are the fruit of all humanities suffering which are pressed to become the wine of Christ's suffering on the cross which in turn is poured out for humanity, transforming all into something holy and life giving the mystical body of Christ."

PAINTING: THE CRUCIFIXION (1991) **'Father into your hands I commend my spirit'. Luke 23.46**

ARTIST – PETER CASSIDY

Peter Cassidy's description of the painting:

"The inspiration for this painting came from this line of scripture. It tries in some small way to capture something of the last moments of Christ's life. The terrible moment of crisis is past **"my God, my God why have you forsaken me" Mark 15.34**, and now Christ forsaken and broken cries out of his Father to embrace Him.

But the painting was also influenced by a book "The passion of our Lord Jesus Christ" written by the French Doctor Pierre Barbet published in the 1950's. Doctor Barbet describes in detail the physical process by which someone dies of crucifixion, and how painful it is for a person to be suspended by the arms with all their body weight pulling down on their arms, stretching them taught like two pieces of string. (I remember as a child being sent to the back of the class and told to hold my arms out for 5 or 10 minutes as a punishment for something or other. That was sore, and it was only the weight of my arms not my whole body!). In a crucifixion the weight and stress on the arms and chest is such that in less than an hour the muscles in the whole upper body, arms, chest, diaphragm, become cramped, locked to the point of making it impossible to breath. Effectively the crucified victim suffocates slowly.

The only way that a person in this appalling situation can stave off death is to try to take as much weight off their arms and onto their legs as possible. For Christ this would have been dreadfully painful being nailed both through the feet and wrists, (the palm of the hand not being strong enough to support the body would rip apart, the nails necessarily would have to pierce the bones of the wrist). So for Christ His time on the cross was foreshortened, but the torture heightened to a continuous excruciating level of pain.

Later on that evening, as the Sabbath approaches the Jews have Pilot break the legs of the two captives. They are still surviving, being only tied and not nailed to their crosses. Now unsupported their bodies soon go into cramp and their final agony cannot be delayed any longer.

This description of the process of dying on a cross made a vivid impression on me. It highlighted all the more the effort which Christ must have made to draw breath enough to be able to speak any words from the cross, and how significant those words must be. He cries out to the Father to embrace his spirit, and so the God, the 'Abba' of love, must have responded to His Son, for Christ Himself had said of a father's love,

> **"Is there anyone among you who would hand his son a stone when he asked for bread,…. How much more will your Father in heaven give good things to those who ask him!" Math. 7: 9/11,**

so the painting includes in the upper half the suggestion of the arrival of the Father to gather into His arms the soul of His Son."

PAINTING: THE RESURRECTION (1998)

ARTIST – PETER CASSIDY

Peter Cassidy's description of the painting:

"The main inspiration for The Resurrection is taken from John's Gospel in which he describes the first meeting Jesus has with anyone after his resurrection, Mary of Magdala, (John 20: 11 to 18). Mary had arrived very early to the tomb on Sunday morning, she is still deeply distraught after the brutal killing of her friend whom she loved. She had wanted to make one last gift to him by anointing his body before the tomb is sealed forever. But there is no body and no Jesus only strangers, (angels), in the tomb. In her confusion she can only cry. After a while she becomes aware of someone approaching her. He is ordinary and unremarkable, she assumes He is the gardener. It's a unique moment of human drama. Here is the risen creator of the world indeed the whole universe, powerful beyond imagination and death, yet in His first meeting with anyone after His death He does not choose to reveal Himself in glory but chooses instead to approach His friend as humbly and unthreateningly as possible. Mary simply mistakes Him for the gardener until He calls her name and then she recognises Him. It is this beautiful moment when Mary's anguish turns to recognition and wonderment that the painting tries in some small way to capture.

Jesus
'I shall draw all people to myself' (J. 12 : 32)
'I am the resurrection' (J. 11 : 25)
'I am the Way, I am the Truth and Life.
No one can come to the Father except
through me' (J. 14 : 6)

Mary of Magdala (John 20 : 11 to 18)

People within the flowers
'All humanity is grass, and all its beauty
like the wild flowers,' (Is. 40 : 6)

The painting depicts more than the meeting of 2 people in a garden. This is a garden of resurrection full of life and rebirth. Unlike many Renaissance or traditional resurrection images which show bodies clambering from graves, (possibly taking inspiration from Ezekiel's words, **'And you will know that I am Lord when I open your graves and raise you from your graves my people', Ez. 37 : 13)**, I have thought instead to interpret the more poetic image of Isaiah, **'All humanity is grass, and all its beauty like the wild flowers', Is. 40 : 6.** which also put me in mind of Jesus' own words, **'and why worry about clothing? Think of the flowers growing in the fields, they never have to work or spin, yet I assure you not even Solomon in all his royal robes was clothed like one of these.' (Matthew 6 : 28).** The people sharing in Christ's resurrection are temporarily lost in death, curled up and withdrawn in themselves, lost in the dandelions and flowers of the garden, they are now called to look outwards, upwards, beyond themselves for Christ proclaims **'I shall draw all people to myself' (J. 12 : 32) 'I am the resurrection' (J. 11 : 25), 'I am the Way, I am the Truth and Life. No one can come to the Father except through me.' (J. 14 : 6).** The people are drawn out of death in the garden through Christ to the everlasting light in the centre of the painting, the rising sun?, the heart of Christ?, to a time and place beyond our ability to understand. Even the leaves of the trees above echo the hosts and multitudes of people whose arms are uplifted in joy to celebrate their resurrection."

FOUR REPRESENTATIONAL STAINED GLASS WINDOWS

ARTIST - PATRICK PYE, MEMBER OF AOSDANA, R.H.A.

1.

2.

3.

4.

FOUR REPRESENTATIONAL STAINED GLASS WINDOWS.

ARTIST – PATRICK PYE, MEMBER OF AOSDANA, R.H.A.

Patrick Pye's description of the Windows:

"1. The first window is the Annunciation, the theme of most theological weight in the series. The disposition of the Angel's entry into the picture may be awkward but was arrived at to emphasise the inwardness of Our Lady's assent. He seems to come from above and behind, interrupting her winding of some wool. The setting is of humble domesticity.

2. The Madonna lies on a sofa attending to the Child. Again an atmosphere of simple and absorbed domesticity.

3. Our Lady in the house of John is the most hieratic of the windows. Here Our Lady is our teacher (our first teacher) and John the humble student. What is our disposition to the extraordinary grace that the Father has bestowed on us in the Son?

4. Baptistry Window: The Baptism of Christ."

GRANITE HOLY WATER FONTS IN CHURCH PORCHES.

The two Holy Water Fonts, which were in the old St. Michael's Church, were replaced by newer ones and made redundant for many years. When the architect of the new Church, the late Mr. Pearse McKenna, discovered them in the grounds of the old Parochial Hall, (now the Boylan Community Centre) he retrieved them and restored them to their former glory and placed one in each porch.

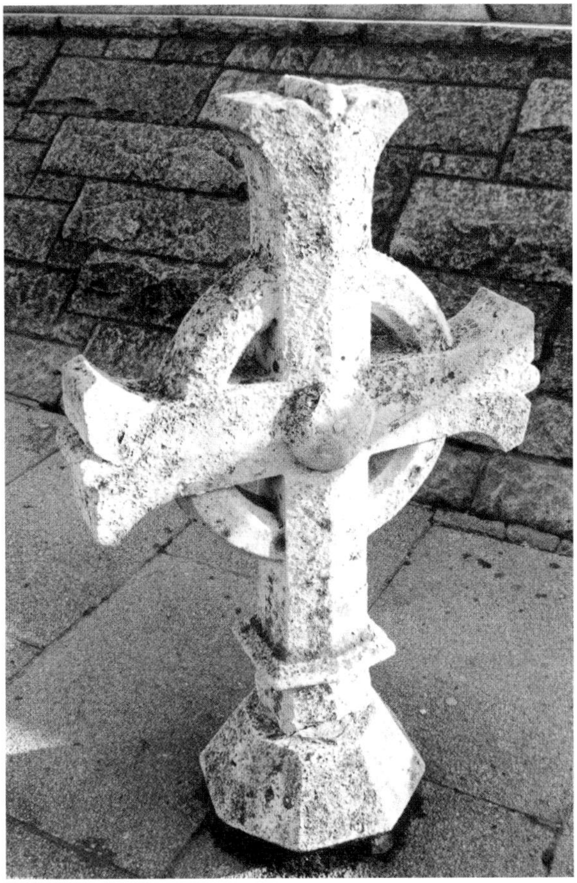

CROSS IN THE CHURCH GROUNDS

The Cross at the rear of the Church near the Church Tower, was removed from the roof of the old church and used to enhance the church grounds.

THE CHURCH TOWER.

A separate publication, prepared by Richard F. Carr, B.M., in 1997, to commemorate the centenary of St. Michael's Church Tower and giving it's history is available by contacting the Parish Office. The lettering on the plaque on the Church Tower wall, is the work of Thomas Glendon, Letter Cutter and Sculptor.

UNMARKED BURIAL SITES WITHIN THE CHURCH.

The remains of three Priests were discovered while excavating the foundations of the new church and were re-interred in bricked graves beneath the Church. The grave of Fr. Thos. O'Sullivan lies roughly beneath the farther area alongside the Baptistry. The first Parish Priest, Canon Sheridan, lies in the Sanctuary area, almost on the site of the Tabernacle and the remains of the second Parish Priest, Canon Cavanagh, lie beneath the Mortuary Exit area – which coincided with the transept area in the old Church.

Special care was taken to ensure that their remains were buried as near as possible to the places where they were discovered.

APPENDIX 1

St. Thérèse of Lisieux 1873 –1897.

Thérèse Martin was born in Alençon in France on 2nd January 1873, the last of nine children, four of whom had already died. Her father was a watchmaker and her mother ran a small lace-making business. When Thérèse was four her mother died and the family moved to Lisieux. Here she spent the next ten years of her life, brought up in an atmosphere of love and affection. Her relationship with her father was one of deepest tenderness and affection. It was this essential experience of love and goodness that opened for her an understanding of the Fatherhood of God. From an early age, she wanted to give herself totally to God, and was devoted to the Eucharist. She struggled with her own stubbornness of will and suffered a lot because of her very sensitive and scrupulous nature. When she was ten years old, she was cured of a mysterious illness through the 'smile of the Queen of Heaven'.

At the age of fifteen, she entered the Carmelite Convent in Lisieux and was given the name 'Thérèse of the Child Jesus'. She spent the next nine years of her life there. Under obedience she also wrote her autobiography, 'The Story of a Soul', which in fact was three different manuscripts, written for three different persons. The first, written in 1895 is addressed to her older sister Pauline, Mother Agnes, who was Prioress at the time. It was meant simply as a 'family souvenir' for her own sisters and contains childhood memories and recollections together with some of her experiences during her first years in the convent.

The second, only three pages of folded paper in very small handwriting, was written the following year for her eldest sister Marie. There is every indication that it was written in great haste and in a state of extreme fatigue. But it is the jewel of all her writings, for in it she reveals the secret of her Little Way and tells of her discovery of her vocation.

The final manuscript is addressed to the new Prioress, Mother Marie de Gonzague. It was written just a few months before Thérèse died, much of it in her invalid chair under the chestnut trees. Thérèse was already in a state of extreme exhaustion and had to finish her writing in pencil, so great was her weakness.

Few saints have had such a profound influence on the spirituality of the twentieth century. Her message is as simple as it is profound. It speaks with gospel clarity and directness to a world weary with its own confusion and complexity. It is a message of hope within despair, of faith within uncertainty; it is the proclamation of the triumph of love as the only ultimate answer to the restless searching of the human heart. Love is at the heart of Thérèse's life and message. Though her life was short, hidden, and for the most part, without social or political dimension, she was fully in tune with the spirit of her age. She asked the same questions, wrestled with the same problems and faced the same pain and anguish as many of her contemporaries. She was one of the first to break the rigid and narrow mould of conservatism that had characterised the nineteenth century. She helped us to return to the Scriptures, deepened our awareness of being part of the Church, and showed us once again the human face of God. She unmasked fear and proclaimed the triumph of love.

As with everything about St. Thérèse there is an originality and a freshness in her understanding of the Blessed Virgin, so different from the sugary and exaggerated presentation of her own day. It is in the Gospels alone that Thérèse finds the real Mary – a woman and a mother who experienced joy and sorrow, hope and disappointment, and lived out her life in faith and love.

St. Thérèse is above all else, the saint of the Gospels. She loved the Gospels, reading them constantly, copying and comparing texts and quoting them effortlessly. In fact her writings contain over a thousand quotations from the Scriptures. She almost knew them by heart, from her constant meditation and reflection on them. She even carried a small copy of the Gospels close to her heart night and day.

When St. Thérèse of the Child Jesus and the Holy Face – the Little Flower – died on 30th September 1897 at the age of twenty-four, she was unknown outside her own convent and a small circle of family and friends. Twenty seven years later almost a million people gathered in Rome for her Canonisation.

Less than three years after her canonisation, St. Thérèse was proclaimed Patroness of the Missions, quite an extraordinary achievement for someone who never set foot on a mission field and who, during her short life knew only a few missionaries, mostly by correspondence. If we ask the secret of her immense influence on the missions we find the answer in her own words: 'It is by prayer and sacrifice alone that we as Carmelites can be useful to the Church.' To Father Roulland (a missionary with whom she corresponded) she said 'This is why I became a Carmelite nun, to be a missionary through love.'

St..Thérèse was declared a Doctor of the Church by Pope John Paul II on the 19th October 1997 – Mission Sunday.

APPENDIX 2

Picture of The Divine Mercy.

Sister Faustina (Helen Kowalska) came from a very poor family in Poland that had struggled hard to make a living on their small farm during World War I. She had only three years of formal education. Hers were the humblest tasks in the convent, usually in the kitchen or the vegetable garden, or as porter.

On February 22nd, 1931, Jesus appeared to Sr. Faustina bringing with Him a message of Mercy for all mankind. In her diary on that date she wrote:

"In the evening, when I was in my cell, I became aware of the Lord Jesus clothed in a white garment. One hand was raised in blessing, the other was touching the garment at the breast. From the opening in the garment at the breast there came forth two large rays, one red, and the other pale. In silence I gazed intently at the Lord. My soul was overwhelmed with fear, but also with great joy. After a while Jesus said to me, 'paint an image according to the pattern you see, with the inscription: "Jesus, I trust in You".'

On October 5th, 1938, St. Faustina died in a convent of the Congregation of Sisters of Our Lady of Mercy in Cracow, Poland.

The Feast of the Divine Mercy is on the first Sunday after Easter. The Novena begins on Good Friday.

Sr. Faustina was canonised by Pope John Paul II on 30th April 2000.

APPENDIX 3

Blessed Edmund Ignatius Rice 1762 – 1844.

Edmund Rice, was born on the 1st June 1762 to Robert and Margaret Rice, prosperous tenant farmers, at Westcourt, Callan, Co. Kilkenny. Despite the Penal Laws against Catholics, the Rice family lived in a comfortable house on a large farm. The nine children, two girls and seven boys, were initially taught at home by travelling teachers. One of these, an Augustinian friar, Fr. Patrick Grace, influenced the children by his holy life and gentle manner. From an early age Edmund had great devotion to the Blessed Sacrament and to Our Lady.

From 1777 he attended a commercial academy in Kilkenny for about two years. In 1779 he began business apprenticeship to his uncle, Michael Rice, in the victualling, provisions and ship-chandling business in Waterford. In 1785 he married Mary Elliott, daughter of a leather merchant. As Michael Rice's sons were not interested in the business it was signed over to Edmund at the age of 24. Tragically, Edmund's wife died as a result of a fall from a horse in 1789, which caused the premature birth of his disabled daughter, Mary. After this personal tragedy, his sister Joan came to housekeep for him and to nurse his daughter. When Mary was fourteen he made financial arrangements for her care by close relatives.

He then turned to providing for the needs of the poor, especially in education. He opened his first school in a converted stable in New Street, Waterford. In 1802 he was joined by two companions, Thomas Grosvenor and Patrick Finn from Callan, and the three began to live a form of community life in the rooms over the stable school. They rose early, prayed together and attended daily Mass. They ate sparingly, taught all day, spent some time in spiritual reading, and prayed again before retiring to bed. This became the blueprint on which the daily lives of the Presentation Brothers and Christian Brothers were based.

On the 7th June, 1803 the three moved to Mount Sion, a purpose-built monastery and school. Near the school, Edmund built a small bakehouse so that he could give the pupils a daily meal of bread and milk. In a loft over the bakehouse, tailors were kept busy making clothes for the boys as well as for other poor people. On August 15th 1808, Edmund and his eight companions took vows according to the Rule of the Presentation Sisters. On that day, Edmund became known as Brother Ignatius in honour of his patron Saint Ignatius of Loyola. Other dioceses heard of the wonderful work being done by the Brothers and suitable young men were sent by their bishops to Mount Sion to train for two and a half years and then return to their native diocese. By now there were foundations in Carrick-on-Suir, Dungarvan, Cork, Dublin, Thurles and Limerick.

In order to allow Edmund to transfer his Brothers from diocese to diocese he was advised to try to amalgamate all houses of his institute under a superior general on the same lines as the Jesuits. On the 5th September 1820, Pope Pius VII approved the Congregation of Christian Brothers. On the Feast of the Holy Name, 20th January, 1822, at the conclusion of a retreat the majority of the Brothers elected Edmund Rice as their Superior General and made their vows as Christian Brothers. A committee, chaired by Edmund, set to work to write a new rule. They studied the rules and constitutions of the Jesuits, the De La Salle Brothers and the Presentation Sisters, and finally compiled a rule which, after a trial period was printed in 1832. Some Brothers stayed with the original rule thus remaining Presentation Brothers.

In 1838 Edmund Rice retired as Superior General. He was then 76 years of age and in poor health. Two years later he made a farewell tour of the Irish schools. In 1841 he became seriously ill and returned to Mount Sion in Waterford where he died on the 29th August 1844.

Brother Rice was pronounced Blessed by Pope John Paul II in October 1996.

Today, the members of the twin congregations of Christian and Presentation Brothers, now spread throughout the world, are happy to honour their common father and founder, Edmund Rice, and to work together for his eventual Canonization.

APPENDIX 4

Blessed Charles of Mount Argus 1821 – 1893.

John Andrew Houben, (Blessed Charles), was born in Munstergeleen, Netherlands, December 11th 1821, and was baptised the same day. He was fourth of a family of eleven children born to Peter and Johanna Houben. The family background was simple and Catholic. They worked in a flour mill owned by their uncle. John's childhood was nothing exceptional. He was shy, quiet, pious, friendly and cheerful, always singing about the house. The one thing in life he wanted was to become a priest. He was a slow learner, and even though he studied well into the early hours he barely scraped through, but persevered. At nineteen he was enrolled for compulsory military service. He was not an outstanding soldier but providentially, it was while in the army he first heard of the Passionists. He joined the Passionists on the 5th November 1845 and on becoming a novice, as was the custom, he had to change his name. Andrew was given the name "Charles". He was ordained a Passionist Priest on 21st December 1850 in Tournai, Belgium. Sadly none of his family could be there. His father had died in August, and his father's long illness meant that the family had no money to make the journey to Tournai for his ordination. He never saw Holland again. He spent the rest of his life in foreign lands speaking a foreign language, for in February 1852 he was sent to England.

It was while in England that he first came in contact with the Irish. A few years later on July 9th 1857 the feast of Our Lady of Hope, he was sent to Ireland to the newly-founded monastery of Mount Argus, in Harold's Cross, Dublin. At the time there were ten Passionists living in a reconstructed farmhouse, who were overworked, discouraged and suffering from malnutrition. They pioneered Christian Doctrine classes in the area and set about building an eighty-roomed monastery and retreat house for priests and lay people, the first of its kind in Ireland.

Charles soon became extraordinarily popular not only in Dublin but all over Ireland, which is probably why he was given a task seldom referred to, namely, collecting money throughout the length and breadth of the country to pay for the new monastery of Mount Argus. Charles was not a good preacher. He never really mastered the language. But it was in the Confessional and in comforting the sick that he excelled. It is his gift of healing which is most clearly recorded. Hundreds of people would come to him to be blessed, as many as three hundred a day, we are told.

After nine years in Mount Argus, he was sent back to England where he remained for eight years. Altogether he laboured for nearly 14 years in England. Not much is known of his work there, except that he took the opportunity to renew himself physically and spiritually. He helped with the novices, did much good work in various parishes and blessed the sick who came to him. However, there is no evidence of any unusual cures.

He was recalled to Mount Argus on January 10, 1874 and there he spent the rest of his life. The Irish people were quick to recognise his sanctity and welcomed his return. Every day hundreds of people came from all parts of Ireland, from England and even from America to Mount Argus to receive his blessing. Many wonderful graces and cures were attributed to his prayers. All revered him as a saint. Charles died at Mount Argus on January 5th, 1893 in his seventy-second year and was buried in the community cemetery.

Charles was beatified by Pope John Paul II on October 16th, 1988.

APPENDIX 5

St. Anthony of Padua 1195-1231.

Ferdinand Bulhom was born in Lisbon, (now Portugal then a part of Spain), on the 15th August, 1195 (13 years after St. Francis of Assisi). His parents, Martin and Maria Bulhom were noble, powerful, and God-fearing people. Having been educated in the Cathedral school, Ferdinand, at the age of fifteen, entered the Order of St. Augustine. After two years he requested to be transferred to the Monastery of the Canons Regular of St. Augustine, in Santa Croce, in Coimbra. There he began eight years of intense study under the Augustinian Rule, which he would later combine with the Franciscan vision. Ferdinand was ordained a priest during this time.

In 1220, the life of the young priest took a crucial turn when the bodies of the first five Franciscan martyrs were returned from Morocco. They had been tortured and beheaded because they continued to preach about Christ despite repeated warnings. Ferdinand was inspired to go to the little Friary in Coimbra and said "Brother, I would gladly put on the habit of your Order if you would promise to send me as soon as possible to the land of the Saracens, that I may gain the crown of the holy martyrs". After some challenges from the Prior of the Augustinians, he was allowed to leave that priory and receive the Franciscan habit, taking the name Anthony. True to their promise, the Franciscans allowed Anthony to go to Morocco, to be a witness for Christ, and a martyr as well. But as often happens, the gift he wanted to give was not the gift that was to be asked of him. He became seriously ill, and after several months realised he had to go home. He never arrived. His ship ran into storms and high winds and was blown east across the Mediterranean. Months later he arrived on the east coast of Sicily. The Friars at nearby Messina, though they didn't know him, welcomed him and began nursing him back to health. Meanwhile he heard from the brethren of Messina that a general chapter was to be held at Assisi, called the Chapter of Mats (so called because the numbers attending were so great, some had to sleep outdoors on mats). He went there, arriving in time to take part in it. The chapter over, Anthony remained, entirely unnoticed. He said nothing of his studies, his only desire was to follow Jesus Christ and so he applied to Father Graziano, Provincial of Coimbra, for a place where he could live in solitude and penance, and enter more fully into the spirit and discipline of Franciscan life. Father Graziano being in need of a priest for the hermitage of Montepaolo (near Forli) sent him there that he might celebrate Mass for the lay people.

Perhaps we would never have heard of Anthony if he hadn't gone to an ordination of Dominican and Franciscan Friars in Forli in 1222. Anthony was asked to give a short sermon. His knowledge was unmistakable, but his holiness was what really impressed everyone there. His quiet life of prayer and penance at the hermitage was exchanged for that of public preacher. St. Francis of Assisi heard of Anthony's previously hidden gifts and Anthony was assigned to preach in Northern Italy and Southern France. In 1224 St. Francis assigned Anthony to teach theology to the Friars. St. Francis wrote "It pleases me that you should teach the friars sacred theology, provided that in such studies they do not destroy the spirit of holy prayer and devotedness, as contained in the Rule". Anthony first taught in a Friary in Bologna, then Montpellier in 1224, and later at Toulouse. He continued to preach as he taught the Friars and assumed more responsibility within the Order. In 1226 he was appointed Provincial Superior of Northern Italy but still found time for contemplative prayer in a small hermitage.

In 1228 he moved to Padua, where he was appointed Provincial. Here he was to continue his teaching and from here he continued to travel in his mission of preaching for the last three years of his short life. In Padua he preached his last and most famous Lenten sermons. The crowds were so great – sometimes 30,000 – that the churches could not hold them, so he went into the piazzas or the open fields. People waited all night to hear him. He needed a bodyguard to protect him from the people armed with scissors who wanted to snip off a piece of his habit as a relic. After his morning Mass and sermon, he would hear confessions. This sometimes lasted all day – as did his fasting.

St. Anthony died in Arcella, near Padua, at the age of thirty-six on 13th June 1231. He had lived fifteen years with his parents, ten years as a Canon Regular of St. Augustine, and eleven years in the Order of Friars Minor. It had been his wish to be buried at Padua and so, despite disputes which arose about possession of his remains, his body was brought in funeral procession on the following Tuesday to the Church of the Franciscan Monastery in Padua. While his remains were conveyed, many miracles took place. From that time Tuesday was therefore chosen as a day especially appropriate for all devotions in honour of St. Anthony.

When the vault in which for thirty years his body had reposed was opened, the flesh was found reduced to dust but the tongue uninjured, fresh, and of a lively red colour. St. Bonaventure, seeing this wonder, exclaimed "O Blessed Tongue that always praised the Lord and made others bless Him, now it is evident what great merit thou hast before God".

St. Anthony was canonized by Pope Gregory IX in 1232.
In 1946 Pope Pius XII officially declared St. Anthony a Doctor of the Universal Church.

STATUES OF ST. ANTHONY.

Since the seventeenth century, artists most often represent the Saint holding the child Jesus in his arms, or with the child standing or seated on a book which the Saint is holding. He is also portrayed holding a lily. These representations are rooted in the miracles associated with them.

With the Child Jesus

While visiting the home of a friend, St. Anthony was praying in his room far into the night when suddenly the room was filled with light more brilliant that the sun. Jesus appeared to St. Anthony in the form of a little child. His friend, awakened and attracted by the brilliant light that filled the house, was drawn with wonder to St. Anthony's room where he witnessed the vision but promised to tell no one of it until after the death of St. Anthony.

With the Lily

This beautiful flower has long been regarded in Christian art as a symbol of purity and integrity of life. In many parts of the world lilies are in bloom in the middle of June when the feast of St. Anthony is observed. The custom of associating the lily with St. Anthony is related to two incidents. On the Saint's feast in 1680, a cut lily had been placed in one of the hands of his statue in a church in Austria. For the whole year, the flower retained its freshness and fragrance. The following year, the stem bore two more lilies, and the church was filled with their fragrance.

The second unusual event took place at Marcasso, on the island of Corsica at the time of the French Revolution. The Franciscans had been forced to leave the island, but the people continued to honour St. Anthony and to invoke his aid as the Friars had taught them. On his feast day, the people set up a shrine for the Saint in a deserted church, and then decorated the Shrine with lilies, roses and other flowers. Many months later, the lilies placed before St. Anthony's statue were found fresh and white while the roses and other floral offerings lay withered and dead.

Holding the Holy Scripture

Saint Anthony is celebrated as a teacher, a preacher and a Scripture Scholar. He was the first teacher in the Franciscan Order, given the special approval and blessing of Saint Francis of Assisi to instruct brother Franciscans. He was an eloquent and effective preacher, calling people back to the faith. In his sermons, he called upon his listeners to live in justice and in peace with one another, constantly using the Scripture, particularly the Gospels.

The Novena to St. Anthony.

This novena is also linked with a legend about a couple in Bologna about the year 1617. The story says that after 22 years of longing for a child the wife took her troubles to St. Anthony. He is said to have appeared to her in a dream telling her "For nine Tuesdays, one after the other, make visits to the church of my Order, on each of those days approach the holy sacraments of penance and of the altar, then pray before my picture and what you ask you shall obtain".

In one version of the story she conceived but gave birth to a badly deformed child. Again, asking the saint's intercession, she touched the child, at St. Anthony's instruction, to his altar, and the deformity at once disappeared.

St. Anthony's Bread.

St. Anthony is today, as he was in his lifetime, the faithful friend of all in trouble, especially the poor and the needy. 'St. Anthony's Bread' means that when a person prays to the saint for a favour, he or she promises to give a gift ('bread') to the poor or some charitable cause. Different legends or stories account for this, one account goes back to 1263. Then, it is said, a child drowned near the Basilica of St. Anthony in Padua, which was still being built. His mother promised that if the child was restored to her she would give for the poor an amount of corn equal to the child's weight. Her prayer and promise were rewarded with the boy's return to life.

Another reason for the practise is traced back to 1890. At that time there lived in Toulon, France, a devout young woman named Louise Bouffier who managed a small bakery store. One morning, Louise could not open the door with her key. Neither could a locksmith, who told her he would have to break the door open. While he went to get his tools, Louise promised St. Anthony she would give some bread to the poor if the door could be opened without force. When the locksmith returned, she begged him to try just once more. The door opened, Louise kept her promise and the poor received bread.

Finder of Lost Things.

The reason for invoking St. Anthony's help in finding lost or stolen things is traced back to an incident in the Saint's own life. Anthony had a book of Psalms that was very important to him. Besides the value of any book before the invention of printing, his prayer book had the notes and comments he had made to use in teaching his students. A novice who had grown tired of living the Franciscan way of life decided to depart from the community. He took with him Anthony's prayer book. Upon realising that his prayer book was missing, Anthony prayed that it would be found or returned to him. In response to Anthony's prayer, the novice was moved to return the prayer book to the Saint and to return to the Order which accepted him back. Shortly after his death, people began praying through Anthony to recover lost or stolen articles.

St. Anthony's Brief (or Letter).

The story is told of a Portuguese woman almost demented by grief and trouble who resolved to put an end to her life by throwing herself into the River Tagus. On her way to the river she stopped to pray before a statue of St. Anthony. During her prayer she fell into a deep sleep. When she awoke she found herself released of her terrible temptation and in her hand this Brief or Letter:

Behold the Cross of the Lord
Begone you enemy powers
The Lion of the tribe of Judah,
The root of David has conquered.
Alleluia.

It has been written that the King wanted to preserve this precious writing, had it brought to him, and placed it in the royal archives, where it is still preserved with the crown jewels of Portugal.

Guardian of the Mails.

The origin of the custom of putting "S.A.G." stamps or writing these initials on envelopes lies in an incident which happened in Spain in 1792. (The letters stand for St. Anthony Guide or Guard). One, Antonio Dante, journeyed to Lima, Peru, leaving his wife behind in Spain. After his departure she wrote to him many times without receiving any reply. Finally she went to a church of St. Francis in Oviedo, and placed in the hands of St. Anthony's statue a letter to her husband in Peru. She prayed that St. Anthony would get the letter to him and obtain a reply. She returned to the chapel the next day. A letter was still clasped in the hands of the statue. She began scolding St. Anthony for not delivering her letter. The noise she made brought the sacristan to her, who said he had tried to get the letter from St. Anthony's hands without success. The wife is then supposed to have reached up and quite easily taken the letter from St. Anthony's hands. At the same time 300 gold coins spilled from the sleeve of the statue. When the letter was opened, it was not the wife's letter but a letter from her husband. He said that not hearing from her for so long he had thought her dead. But now her most recent letter had been delivered by a Franciscan priest and he was sending his reply through that same Friar.

APPENDIX 6

THE ORGAN IN ST. MICHAEL'S CHURCH, DUN LAOGHAIRE, CO. DUBLIN

BUILT BY RIEGER ORGANS, AUSTRIA, AND INSTALLED IN 1974. (MECHANICAL ACTION)

STOP LIST:

PEDAL

1. Principal 16'
2. Subbass 16'
3. Octav 8'
4. Gedackt 8'
5. Choralbass 4'
6. Hintersatz IV 2 2/3'
7. Fagott 16'
8. Schalmei 4'

HAUPTWERK

1. Pommer 16'
2. Principal 8'
3. Rohrflöte 8'
4. Octav 4'
5. Sesquialter II 2 2/3'
6. Superoctav 2'
7. Mixtur VI 1 1/3'
8. Trompete Spanisch 8'
   Tremulant

BRUSTWERK

1. Salicional 8'
2. Holzgedackt 8'
3. Principal 4'
4. Koppelflöte 4'
5. Gemshorn 2'
6. Quintlein 1 1/3'
7. Zimbel III 1/2'
8. Regal 16'
9. Krummhorn 8'
   Tremulant
   Expression

KOPPELN

II/I, I/P, II/P

KEY TO MAP

	Name of Artist	Location Number on Map
CHURCH EXTERIOR		
The Church Tower.		
The external walls of the Church are faced with granite, supplied from the remains of the old Church.		
The Cross at the rear of Church near the Church Tower is from the roof of the old Church.		
St. Michael above main entrance	Imogen Stuart	1
Fixed Panel on Main Door	Imogen Stuart	2
Handrails on Main Doors	Imogen Stuart	3
Short handles on side doors – 3	Imogen Stuart	4,5,6
CHURCH INTERIOR		
<u>Porch (Marine Road)</u>		
Dalle-du-Verre Glass Window	Murphy Devitt Studios	7
Granite Holy Water Font		8
<u>Baptistry – Sunken Area</u>		
Painting of Baptism	Peter Cassidy	9
Baptism of Christ Stained Glass Window	Patrick Pye	10
Baptismal Font	The late Michael Biggs	11
Tapestry of Our Lady and the Child Jesus	Eoin and Pat Butler	12
The Abstract Stained Glass Windows	Murphy Devitt Studios	Throughout
Statue of the Sacred Heart.	Carved in Oberammergau	14
Organ	Rieger Organs	15
Tabernacle Pillar	The late Michael Biggs	16
Tabernacle	The late Richard E. King	17
Tabernacle behind pillar	The late Richard E. King	18
Sanctuary Lamp	The late Richard E. King	19
Tapestry on Sanctuary Wall	Owen and Pat Butler	20
Statue of Our Lady	Carved in Oberammergau	21
Statue of St. Thérèse of Lisieux	Unknown	22
Bell	Unknown	23

KEY TO MAP

	Name of Artist	Location Number on Map
Mortuary		
Crucifix in Mortuary	Unknown	24
Statue of St. Joseph	Unknown	25
Side Chapel		
Picture of Divine Mercy	Unknown	26
Statue of Blessed Charles of Mount Argus	The late Peter J. Brennan	27
Statue of Blesssed Edmund Ignatius Rice	The late Peter Grant	28
Side Chapel		
Statue of St. Anthony of Padua	Carved in Oberammergau	29
Porch Eblana Avenue.		
Granite Holy Water Font		30
Dalle-du-Verre Glass Window	Murphy Devitt Studios	31
Painting over Confessional	Unknown	32
Plaque of 4th Station	Ian Stuart	33
Holy Water Font	Unknown	34
Fourteen Stations of the Cross	The late Madame Jammet	35
Paintings		
The Last Supper	Peter Cassidy	36
The Crucifixion	Peter Cassidy	37
The Resurrection	Peter Cassidy	38
Representational Stained Glass Windows		
Annunciation	Patrick Pye	39
Madonna with Child	Patrick Pye	40
Our Lady and St. John	Patrick Pye	41
Holy Water Font.	Unknown	42
High Altar	The late Michael Biggs	43
Ambo	The late Michael Biggs	44
Seat	The late Michael Biggs	45
Crucifix	The late Richard E.King	46
Mounted on Liscanor Slate from Co. Clare		47
Altar Bell (used during Mass)	Imogen Stuart	48

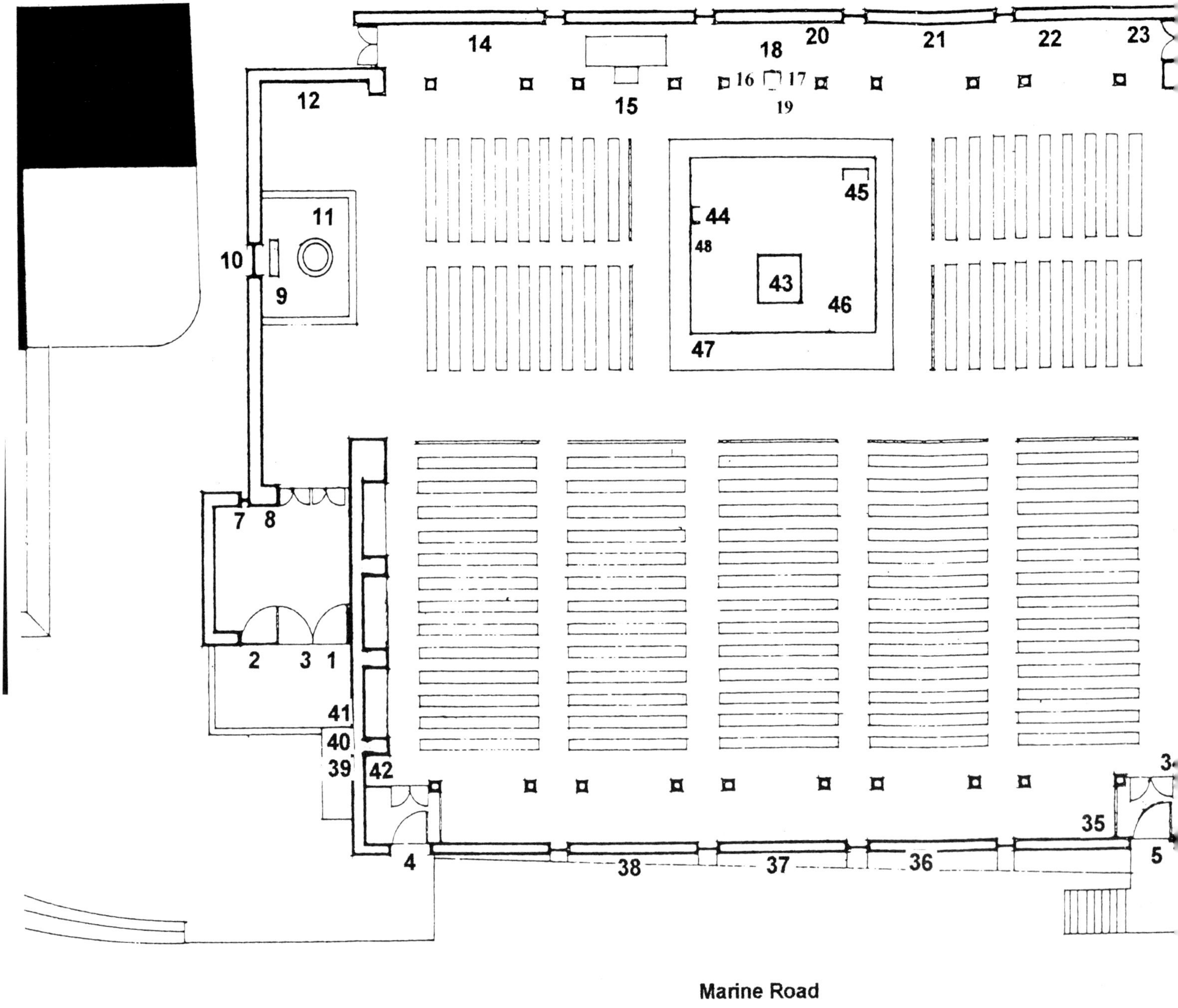
14
18
20
21
22
23
12
15
16
17
19
11
10
9
45
44
48
43
46
47
7
8
2
3
1
41
40
39
42
4
38
37
36
35
5
Marine Road

Map of Church

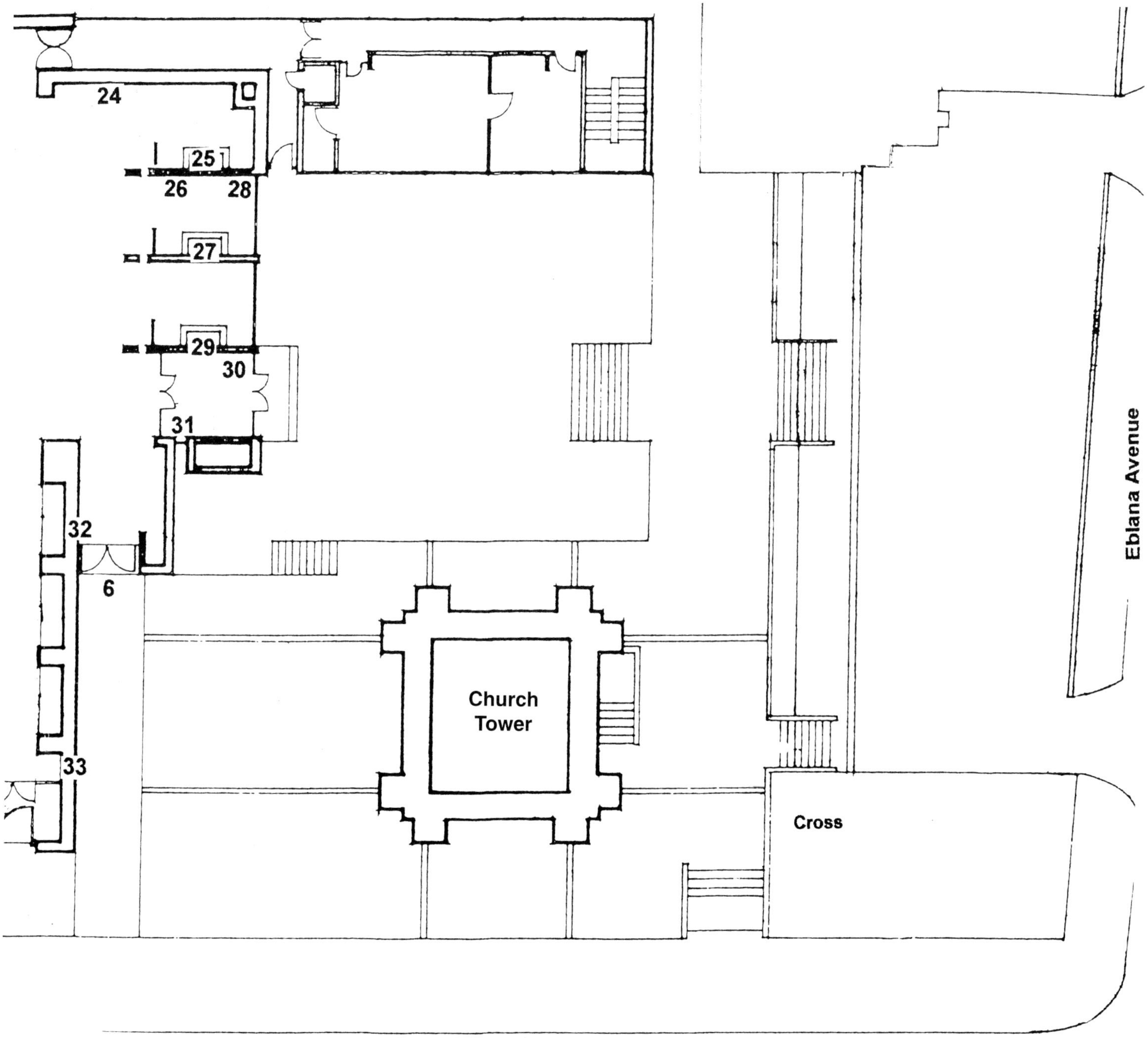